Contents

A new American president

In January 2017 a controversial new president moved into the White House in Washington, DC. His name was Donald Trump. Mr Trump was well-known as a businessman and TV star. But now he would be leader of the United States!

President
Donald
Trump

by Nick Robison

FALKIRK COMMUNITY
TRUST LIBRARIES

raintree

a Capstone company — publishers for children

Raintree is an imprint of Capstone Global Library Limited, a company incorporated in England and Wales having its registered office at 264 Banbury Road, Oxford, OX2 7DY – Registered company number: 6695582

www.raintree.co.uk
myorders@raintree.co.uk

Editorial Credits
Jessica Nelson, designer; Scott Burger, media researcher

Photo Credits
AP Photo: Mike Groll, 9; Getty Images: New York Daily News Archive, 13, Stringer/Amanda Edwards, 17, Stringer/Kena Betancur, cover; Newscom: AdMedia/CNP/Ron Sachs, 23, Reuters/Brendan McDermid, 19, Sipa USA/Anthony Behar, 29, ZUMA Press/Judie Burstein, 7; Shutterstock: Andrea Izzotti, 5, Christopher Halloran, 21, Evan El-Amin, 1, jiawangkun, 15, Joseph Sohm, 25, Lev Radin, 27, SINITAR, 11

ISBN 978 1 4747 5509 2 (hardback)
21 20 19 18 17
10 9 8 7 6 5 4 3 2 1

ISBN 978 1 4747 5512 2 (paperback)
22 21 20 19 18
10 9 8 7 6 5 4 3 2 1

British Library Cataloguing in Publication Data
A full catalogue record for this book is available from the British Library.

Printed and bound in India.

American presidents live and work in the White House in Washington, DC.

Born into business

Donald Trump was born in
New York City on 14 June 1946.
He was the fourth of five children.
Donald's father, Frederick,
ran a company that built
apartment buildings. His mother,
Mary, worked with various charities.

Born in New
York City

1946

Donald (centre) with his father, Frederick, and his mother, Mary

When he was 13, Donald's parents
sent him to a military school in
New York. The school helped
Donald set and reach goals.
He also enjoyed playing
baseball, football and
other sports at the school.

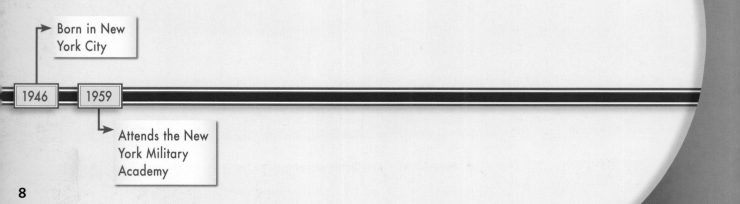

Born in New
York City

1946

1959

Attends the New
York Military
Academy

Donald in the 1964 yearbook from the New York Military Academy

After military school, Donald
went to Fordham University in
New York. Later he went to
the Wharton School of the
University of Pennsylvania.
In 1968, Donald earned a
university degree in economics.

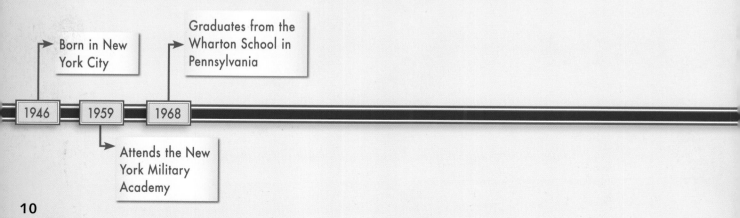

Born in New
York City

Graduates from the
Wharton School in
Pennsylvania

1946   1959   1968

Attends the New
York Military
Academy

The Wharton School in Pennsylvania

The business world

In 1971, Donald took over his father's business. Soon he renamed it The Trump Organization. He bought, sold and constructed many buildings. These included office buildings, hotels and resorts. Donald earned a lot of money.

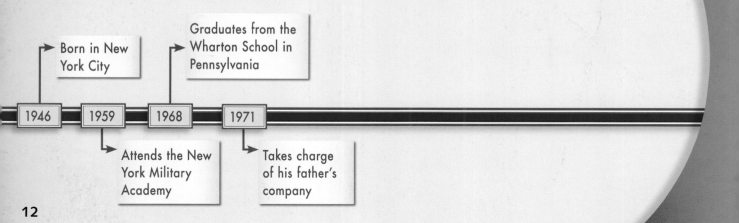

Born in New York City

Graduates from the Wharton School in Pennsylvania

| 1946 | 1959 | 1968 | 1971 |

Attends the New York Military Academy

Takes charge of his father's company

Donald announces plans for a convention centre in New York in 1977.

Donald owns many fancy buildings
in the United States and around
the world. Many of the buildings
have his last name on them.
Donald has also written several
books about business and his life.

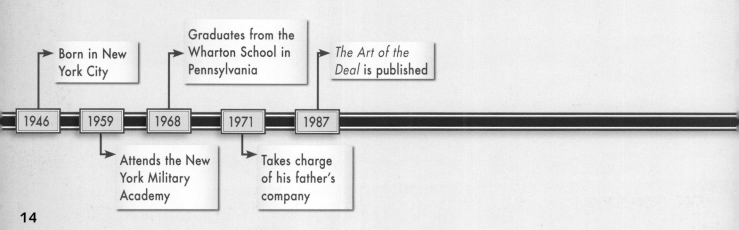

Born in New
York City

Graduates from the
Wharton School in
Pennsylvania

The Art of the Deal is published

| 1946 | 1959 | 1968 | 1971 | 1987 |

Attends the New
York Military
Academy

Takes charge
of his father's
company

The main entrance to Trump Tower on Fifth Avenue in New York City

Donald also became a
famous entertainer.
He starred in his own reality
TV show, *The Apprentice*.
In the show, people tried to win
a job working for Donald.

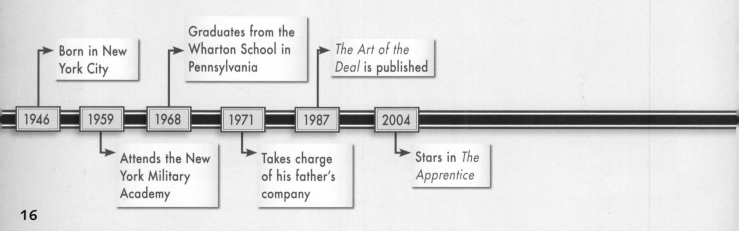

Born in New
York City

Graduates from the
Wharton School in
Pennsylvania

*The Art of the
Deal* is published

| 1946 | 1959 | 1968 | 1971 | 1987 | 2004 |

Attends the New
York Military
Academy

Takes charge
of his father's
company

Stars in *The
Apprentice*

Family life

Donald Trump has been married three times. He has five children. He married his current wife, Melania, in 2005. She used to be a model.

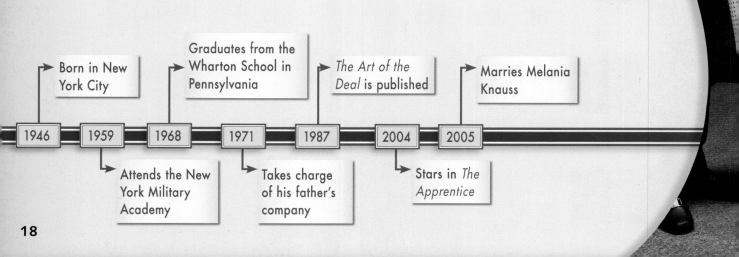

Born in New York City

Graduates from the Wharton School in Pennsylvania

The Art of the Deal is published

Marries Melania Knauss

| 1946 | 1959 | 1968 | 1971 | 1987 | 2004 | 2005 |

Attends the New York Military Academy

Takes charge of his father's company

Stars in *The Apprentice*

Donald Trump with his family

Change to politics

Over time, Donald became interested in politics. He thought about running for president several times. He also thought about running for governor of New York in 2006 and 2014.

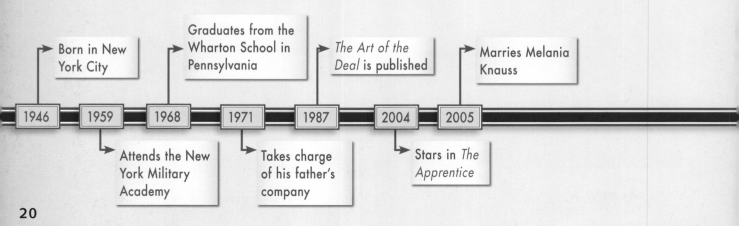

Born in New York City

Graduates from the Wharton School in Pennsylvania

The Art of the Deal is published

Marries Melania Knauss

| 1946 | 1959 | 1968 | 1971 | 1987 | 2004 | 2005 |

Attends the New York Military Academy

Takes charge of his father's company

Stars in *The Apprentice*

Donald ran for president in 2016 as a candidate for the Republican Party. He had never held a political position before. He formed a team to help him win the campaign.

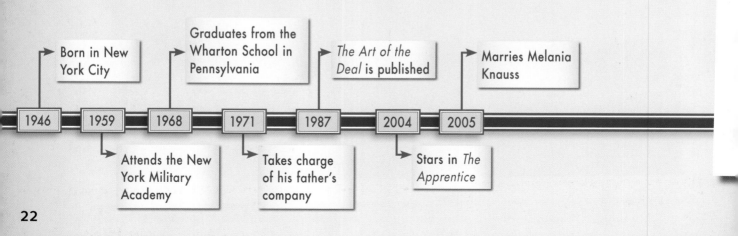

Born in New York City

Graduates from the Wharton School in Pennsylvania

The Art of the Deal is published

Marries Melania Knauss

1946 | 1959 | 1968 | 1971 | 1987 | 2004 | 2005

Attends the New York Military Academy

Takes charge of his father's company

Stars in *The Apprentice*

In July 2016, Donald Trump became the Republican presidential candidate.

Donald talked about making
more jobs available for workers.
He also covered health care,
keeping Americans safe
and many other topics.
His supporters were excited about
the changes he planned to make.

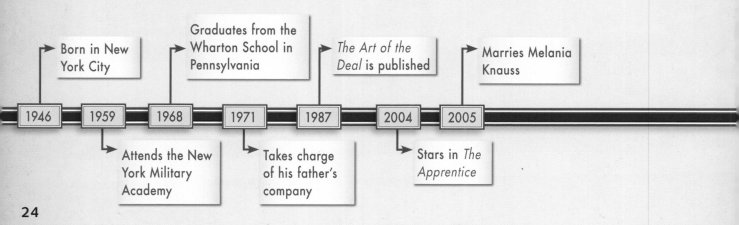

Born in New
York City

Graduates from the
Wharton School in
Pennsylvania

*The Art of the
Deal* is published

Marries Melania
Knauss

1946   1959   1968   1971   1987   2004   2005

Attends the New
York Military
Academy

Takes charge
of his father's
company

Stars in *The
Apprentice*

Winning the election

Americans voted on
8 November 2016.
The next day, it was announced
that Donald had won the election.
He gave an acceptance speech
in New York. The large crowd
chanted, "USA! USA!"

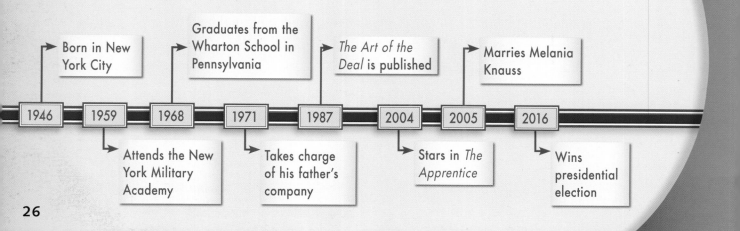

1946 — Born in New York City

1959 — Attends the New York Military Academy

1968 — Graduates from the Wharton School in Pennsylvania

1971 — Takes charge of his father's company

1987 — *The Art of the Deal* is published

2004 — Stars in *The Apprentice*

2005 — Marries Melania Knauss

2016 — Wins presidential election

Donald gives a victory speech next to his wife, Melania, and son Barron.

President Trump

Donald Trump became the 45th American president on 20 January 2017. His slogan during the campaign was "Make America Great Again". It will be interesting to see what Donald can do to make that happen.

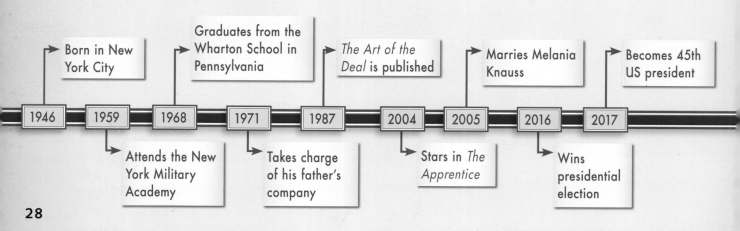

Born in New York City

Graduates from the Wharton School in Pennsylvania

The Art of the Deal is published

Marries Melania Knauss

Becomes 45th US president

| 1946 | 1959 | 1968 | 1971 | 1987 | 2004 | 2005 | 2016 | 2017 |

Attends the New York Military Academy

Takes charge of his father's company

Stars in *The Apprentice*

Wins presidential election

Donald Trump is sworn in as the 45th president of the United States.

Facts about Donald Trump

Born:
14 June 1946

Parents:
Frederick and Mary Trump

Marriages:
Ivana Zelnícková (1977–1992)
Marla Maples (1993–1999)
Melania Knauss (2005–present)

Children:
Donald Jr, born in 1977 (with Ivana Zelnícková)
Ivanka, born in 1981 (with Ivana Zelnícková)
Eric, born in 1984 (with Ivana Zelnícková)
Tiffany, born in 1993 (with Marla Maples)
Barron, born in 2006 (with Melania Knauss)

Favourite films:
Donald has many favourite films, including
Citizen Kane and *The Godfather*.

Favourite sport:
Golf

Nickname:
The Donald

Glossary

acceptance speech speech a politician gives when he or she wins an election

campaign actions taken towards a specific goal, such as winning an election

candidate person who runs for office, such as president

charity group that helps people in need

controversial something that lots of people disagree with

election act of choosing someone or deciding something by voting

governor person elected to be the head of a state's government in the United States

reality TV TV show without any scripts or professional actors

vote to make a choice in an election

Index